Copyright © 2013 Joseph Bronner

Draft2Digital Edition

I0474576

Draft2Digial Edition License Notes

This book is licensed for your personal enjoyment only.
This book may not be re-sold or given away to other
people. If you would like to share this book with another
person, please purchase an additional copy for each
person you share it with. If you're reading this book and
did not purchase it, or it was not purchased for your use
only, then you should return to any publishing website at
which it is sold and purchase your own copy. Thank you
for respecting the author's work.

Disclaimer:

This book is <u>not</u> intended as advice. Please be advised: you are 100% responsible for all trades made in penny stocks, or any stocks in the stock market, and you should seek professional investment assistance before trading even a penny in the stock market. When investing, especially in penny stocks, you should be fully prepared to lose <u>everything!</u> The characters and events in this book are 100% real, although some of the book's features are enhanced for reading pleasure and the names of included persons and their respective associations are changed to protect their privacy.

By reading any further, you release the author and any connections to him or the book from any obligations or liabilities to your own trading, and furthermore, you agree not to bring any legal action against the author or any connections to him or the book for any losses incurred from your own trading or anyone who trades on your behalf or from any advice given by you based on this book.

Please see the definitions' page towards the end for a full description of trading terms.

Prologue

His hands sweaty and his heart pounding, The Student typed in his first buy order in the penny stock world. He clicked on the CHOP ticker and hit the buy button. In the shares section he typed 10, changed the order to limit and set his price at $2.95, and put the order in as good for one day. Taking a deep breath, his sweaty finger pressed down the mouse pad on his lap top and clicked the submit button.

His life will never be the same again...

Into a world full of people out to steal his money, The Student thrust himself full forcibly. Feeling his back against the wall having to pay back student loans, he decided to try his hand at penny stock trading. In this vortex of relentless money hungry penny stock manipulators, The Student finds himself an island of security on a Board that provides him with safe and secure trades. Or is this safety and security just a new age scam that gives him a false sense of confidence as the manipulators secretly and slowly milk him to his last penny? Follow The Student through his quest to gather riches and pay off his college debts. Will he succeed in making a fortune or will he fall into the traps of suspecting scammers and plunge into the bleak darkness of bankruptcy, or still further, will it all just be in vain?

Chapter 1 – The Trader

The Student is a hardworking and an educated man. He believes that the way a person does anything is the way that person does everything. However, he has made many mistakes in his life for which he is grateful. But being grateful has not made him rich. Being financially well off, in the sense that he can do whatever he wants whenever he wants without being held down by a "job", is one of his most desirable life goals. Therefore, from his mistakes, The Student has found a plethora of useful wisdom and knowledge which he uses to help him in all aspects of life.

The Student is also a fulltime student. He has been one for quite some time now. In the beginning, he did not know what he wanted to do, except work in healthcare. So he just took the classes that most healthcare degrees required. Before he knew it, he had changed his major five times and had now decided on a career path. But he knew he had an uphill battle and that his chosen path was going to leave him without a job for 26 months while he attended the University. But his strong desire to help people has fed his unrelenting tenacity that has been forcing him to put in long hours at work and school in order to accomplish his dreams. But, at the same time, the long tenure he has endured in school has left him with insufficient funds; which are not nearly enough to carry him through graduate school.

It was in his final semester of undergraduate school that he discovered penny stock trading. He was browsing success and money videos on youtube.com and found a short video on penny stock trading. It was a video about a normal guy who, through discovering the "secrets" of penny stock trading, took a few hundred bucks and turned it into a million in a few years (or so he said).

This strongly interested The Student and he took it upon himself to do a little more research on the subject. And the more he looked into it, the more he found people who said they made tons of money by trading penny stocks on online websites such as Etrade, TD Ameritrade, and Scottrade.

Once The Student felt like he had gathered enough information on penny stock trading, he searched for the cheapest website to join so that he could try his hand at this miraculous discovery. The cheapest website he could find was TradeKing. However, he soon found that although the website was the cheapest (five dollars per trade rather than the standard eight to ten dollars per trade), it did not allow him to trade penny stocks.

Frustrated, The Student left TradeKing for Etrade. After his account was fully transferred, he proceeded to fund it. He knew that this was going to be a learning curve, so he started with just a grand. For buying something, a thousand dollars can be a lot of money. But in the stock trading world, a thousand dollars is nothing. This he will find out later.

Through the YouTube videos, The Student discovered a website where traders would share information. *Ihub.com* was soon bookmarked as was stockcharts.com, etrade.com and a few other charting websites along with a few "pump" documenting websites. A "pump" is a moniker which describes how a company, or an outside source, can pay other companies, websites or people to promote their stock. These entities we will call pumpers. Pumpers can be paid, which is most common, or free volunteer pumpers.

Once a pump is on, the company's stock is promoted with various means. Most of the time, it is successful and penny stock traders invest their capital into that stock.

Then the company releases news and more people invest their money. Well, after the "pump" comes the inevitable "dump". Those who got in early and who have seen their price per share (PPS) rise dramatically, now start to sell off. The PPS then begins to drop. As the PPS drops, those investors who bought in later thinking they were going to make a quick buck start to freak out. Their emotions get the better of them and they sell, some for a little profit, some for a break even trade, some for a little loss, and others for a huge substantial loss. Sometimes these "pumps" take weeks to reach a desired percentage increase. But the "dump" can happen in a matter of seconds.

There is also front loading. Front loading is when a group of investors pour their money into a stock that has an extremely low PPS. Then they alert the stock ticker (symbol) to their subscribers. As their subscribers begin to pour their money into this company, the PPS rises dramatically. So let's say the front loaders buy a ticker for a price of .0002 PPS. This brings the price to .0004. Then the front loaders alert it to their subscribers. The subscribers, upon seeing the PPS has already risen 100%, buy into it. The stock then rises another 200% in PPS to .0012. Then all of the front loaders sell their shares at a price of .001 and since they were holding the majority of shares, the front loaders make all the profit and the PPS plummets (the "dump") and most of their subscribers lose most of their money.

However, most penny stock tickers have a second run. Those who missed the first huge PPS percentage increase, will try to push the PPS back up with buys. If they are unsuccessful at maintaining the increase in PPS, it will slowly but surely come back down to its original price of .0002.

Chapter 2 – Beginner Trading

The Student bought his first stock ever via an internet trading platform (TradeKing) at one dollar and five cents per share. He was just learning what he was doing. So he realized that buying only 10 shares with a commission of $4.95 an order would not net him any profits unless the stock he bought jumped to roughly one dollar and ninety cents a share. This would give him a dollar profit. Nonetheless, he bought this stock anyway just to get the experience.

The stock he bought, CYTK, climbed to one dollar and nine cents a share in roughly two months. The Student decided to sell this stock just before he transferred his account to Etrade. He just got so frustrated because TradeKing had a limit on pink sheets and over the counter stocks. TradeKing blocked most trading in these low priced stocks due to what they called "unforeseen trade charges that could run in the thousands of dollars". So he was unable to trade most of what he wanted, which were stocks under a penny. What a joke!

Pink sheet stocks (PK) and over the counter stocks (OTC) are stocks that do not trade in a common stock exchange, such as the NASDAQ or New York Stock Exchange (NYSE), among others. Therefore, before transferring his account to Etrade, The Student went ahead and bought a few shares of Disney (DIS) and Birkshire Hathoway (BRK.B) because he was able to trade for $4.95 a trade with TradeKing, while Etrade charges $9.99 a trade. Then he called Etrade and sent in the necessary documents in order to get his account fully transferred to Etrade. The entire process took about a week and a half.

Now that his account was fully transferred, The Student was ready to get into his penny stock trading business.

Through talking to a few people about his interest, he found out that one of his friends, The Doctor, also traded stocks. So, they started exchanging information and philosophies. The Doctor's philosophy was to jump in at the open on a stock that is soaring and to ride it until he felt ready to sell. However, avoiding the open is something that The Student soon learned was wise to do.

Unfortunately for him, The Student's penny stock trading business, like many other startup businesses, lost money. Initially, he traded with his friend, The Doctor, by buying a stock at the open. However, because he was new at the volatility of these penny stocks, he let his emotions take control of him and he sold at the worst of times.

His first month of trading was in April. During this time, he lost 20% on FITXD, 18% on HIDC, 98% on LBTG, 58% on PUNL, 27% on AMBS and 29% on REVI. He lost all these percentages by buying in as the stock was soaring and watching it immediately reverse its fortunes. Later, The Student learned that all of these stocks were paid promotions and that he should have never bought into them.

During this time, however, he happened to find a message board on ihub.com called The Mayor Board. Before he actually let down his defenses and trusted the board, he actually put it on his ignore list, especially The Mayor. On the ihub's main page, there is a twitter feed which reposts all messages that are posted on respective boards. The Mayor Board was one of those boards. The Mayor's posts were one of the main posts that were tweeted on this twitter feed. So The Student naturally thought that The Mayor was just pumping his own stocks. He later found this to be the most unwise deduction that a person in his position could have made.

Because of The Mayor and the Board, during this month of April, even though he lost a total of $300.00 on his trades, The Student was still up $80. And this is how: since The Student was a newbie, he knew he was going to lose money in the beginning. So he only funded his account with $1200. First he deposited $500, then anther $300 and then finally another $400 was added as he continued to lose money. However, each trade that he made was no more than $150.00 per stock. Although trading in such small amounts makes it harder to lose money, it also makes it harder to make money. At a hundred dollar buy in, the stock, at $9.99 per trade (let's say ten dollars to make it simple and that's ten dollars to buy and ten dollars to sell), a stock would have to rise 20% just to break even. Even in the penny stock world, 20% does not always happen right away nor does it always go in the buyer's favor, which is something The Student learned the hard way.

Now, onto The Mayor and the Board's saving grace; there were three plays which The Mayor alerted to his Mayor Board that made The Student money and kept him out of the red. Red means actually losing money. These stocks were REAC on which he made 121%, MPIX on which he made 49% and TDEY on which he made 115%. And this brought his grand total to positive eighty dollars, meaning $80 in the green.

Unfortunately for The Mayor, there were many attackers on ihub who accused him of being a pumper. Once a penny stock rises to hundreds and thousands of a percent, it is bound to get exhausted and collapse. This very situation happened to REAC. It ran up to about 130% (.03 PPS) and then within minutes it crashed all the way down to .01 PPS, only to settle at about .014 PPS. Those that bought high thinking it would keep going up, chastised those who initially alerted the stock ticker. The

Student himself had been a victim of this penny stock volatility. But not this time; he got out almost right at the top. So he was beginning to learn the game.

REAC was the stock ticker which provoked The Student to call the The Mayor Board home. But not every alert made him money. The Student still had a long way to go before he truly learned the game. He felt like he learned a lot. He knew how to read level II (L2), which shows how many shares were being bid and for what price and how many shares are being sold on the ask and for what price. He also knew how to read charts and interpret technical analysis. But somehow, he missed one of the most crucial pieces to penny stock trading.

Chapter 3 – The Mayor Board

It wasn't long after trading with The Mayor and the Board
that The Student found himself making up for the full
breadth of losses he attained. One key to trading that The
Student soon learned is patience. There were two alerts by
The Mayor that The Student bought into. These tickers
were WPNV and FLPC. The Student bought these and
waited. Months went by with no action. There was no
volume and no volatility. The stock prices would drop a
few percentages and then rise a few percentages. But
eventually the PPS would find its way back to his original
buy in price. This frustrated him and in his annoyance,
The Student sold WPNV. The day after he sold it, it rose
50%! Now The Student was angry. He held FLPC another
week. Then he decided that he sold the wrong ticker and
he should have held onto WPNV. He felt like FLPC was a
dead duck. So he sold it. Literally, the day after he sold it,
FLPC jumped up over 40%+! After these experiences, he
knew the stock market was singling him out. Somehow
the computers knew when he sold his shares and decided
to explode the PPS up to new highs.

FLPC and WPNV taught The Student two of the most
valuable lessons in penny stock trading. They are patience
and trusting one's self. He vowed to never again give up on
a penny stock trading play and to start buying in with
more than hundred dollars a trade. The first lesson only
applies if one does not buy in at the top. That would be
the worst rule in the world to follow if one were to buy at
the top. That will quickly bleed the money right out of a
trader's account.

It was about this time that The Student bought in MPIX,
another Mayor alert. He bought in with more money than
his previous buy-ins on other stocks and it actually made
him a nice little profit. There were a few other tickers that

he bought via the The Mayor Board that made him some money. But then came the big turd. This ticker was the only call by The Mayor that The Student found himself regretting. But even then it was because he still had not fully understood the word "patience".

On the ECOS board in ihub, the Board was shunned and rejected. Every long term investor, save one or two, were morally attacking The Mayor and his followers for ruining their investments. Some called him a scammer, others called him a pumper and accused the him of tarnishing an otherwise top flight investment. The stock ticker PPS was below a penny at the time. The Mayor and his fellow traders sent it up a good 50%, but it never gained full steam. The Student pulled out almost immediately and sent over stern but respectful posts to those who rejected his presence. He was part of the Mayor Traders. So by rejecting the Mayor and his board members, those investors were also rejecting The Student. He told them he was removing his position from the stock and if they were smart, they would have just rode the PPS jump and sold for profit, then bought back in once the PPS dropped back to its original position. There were a couple of investors that had the presence to do just that and actually thanked the Board for their attendance on the board.

ECOS was truly the only Board hiccup, or so The Student thought. He bought in at .0005 and watched as the ticker dropped in PPS to .0002. And as soon as it rebounded back to .0005, The Student sold it. However, if The Student would have held onto it for another month and a half, that is until about mid November, he would have realized about a 300% gain as it ran up to .015 PPS.

The Student was also able to trade TDEY three times for multiple 50% gains, MPIX for two 50% gains and MINE for three 50% gains. Each time, these stocks would hold a portion of its gains. Then the stock chart would reset and the stock would rise again. TDEY, for example, started at .0005 PPS, ran up to .0012 PPS, reset to .0008 PPS, then ran to .005 PPS .

As The Student was making money off of The Mayor's due diligence (DD) and the Board's backing of his alerts, he began to notice the most crucial key in stock trading. This is the pattern. See, every stock ticker in penny land has a pattern. For instance, TDEY, its current pattern is trading from .0008 PPS to .0012 PPS, for a gain of 50%. This was before its breakout to .005 PPS. Once The Student saw the pattern, he would bid sit (this is what traders call placing a bid and waiting for it to be filled) at .0008 PPS. Once his bid was filled, which there is no guaranteeing that it would be, he would then immediately place a sell order for .0012 PPS (this is called "setting the sell", a term he learned from The Mayor). Then once someone buys at that price, his sell order would be filled and he could rinse and repeat. This is pattern trading, which his very successful.

The Mayor Board continues to be The Student's saving grace and trading home. Everything alerted here is worth taking a look at, which The Mayor recommends. He always reminds his followers and board members to always seek professional investment advice and to do his or her own DD before trading the ticker.

The Student sees The Mayor and The Mayor Board as his northern star guiding his way through the foggy penny stock trading world. And that light is always shining.

Chapter 4 – Trading Rules

There are 20 rules or guidelines on the THE MAYOR BOARD on ihub that The Student now uses to trade. These rules and interpretations are as follows:

1. History repeats itself (pattern trading)

2. People drive buying and selling (emotion)

3. Buy at Support and Sell at Resistance (these can be seen on the chart)

4. Short rallies not sell offs (The Trader doesn't short, so this is irrelevant to him)

5. Do not buy into a major moving average or sell into one (oops!)

6. Do not chase momentum (which is what The Trader did in the beginning)

7. Exhaustion gaps get filled

8. Trends test the point of last resistance and/or support

9. Trade with the tick, not against it

10. If the trader has to look, it isn't there

11. Sell the second high, buy the second low

12. The trend is the trader's friend in the last hour (power hour)

13. Avoid the open (oops!) [The open is when the stock exchange opens in the AM]

14. Downtrends reverse after a top, two lower highs, and a double bottom (chart)

15. Buyers (Bulls) live above the 200 MA Sellers (Bears) live below it (moving average)

16. Price has a memory

17. Big volume kills moves by causing the ticker to trade sideways (equal buying and selling)

18. Trends never turn on a dime

19. Bottoms take longer to form than tops

20. Beat the crowd into and out of the door

These are all The Mayor's rules which all PK and OTC stock traders should live by. If The Student found these rules earlier, he would be in the green. But as it stands, he is down only a few hundred bucks, which is a far cry from being down almost 60% of his total investment. But by following the above rules, picking which Mayor alerts he wants to play, and trading accordingly, The Student has been making great gains and is almost even.

During his current success streak, The Student also met another trader via Facebook, The Professor. The Professor is an interesting man and like The Student, he is more than willing to lend a hand and share his advice.

The Professor's specialty was to find stock tickers that were trading in a very low range. He would buy the bottom and ride it a little way up. One of the best tips that The Professor shared with The Student was to buy a stock that is being sold at .0001. For this, he would have to "bid sit" for up to three weeks. Then once the order is filled, The Student would set his sale at .0002. That's a 100% gain and an 80% profit.

To "bid sit" means to place a bid for a stock at a certain price and to make it good for up to sixty days. Then the bid would stay on that stock at that price until it either is filled, is canceled, or until it expires.

Of course, The Student was skeptical at first. But his first successful trade at this level was with a stock with the ticker symbol WRIT. The Student purchased 1,490,000 shares of this stock at .0001 in two 745,000 share buys. He then sold them all at .0002 for a 70% profit (since there were two buys, there were two buy commission fees and one sell commission fee of $9.99 each). The total purchase price was $178.00 and the sell was for $288.00. That's a nice $110.00 profit, chump change for billionaires, but a good gain for a college student who is playing with disposable income.

The Student posted on THE MAYOR BOARD for buy-in advice. He got one reply. The trader suggested that he purchase for no less than $300.000. However, when it comes to .0001 plays, The Student decided to play it safe and keep his buy-ins low.

Stocks trading that low are VERY risky. The greatest risk is a reverse split (R/S). When an R/S happens, a company will make a certain number of shares equal to a lesser number of shares. And then the PPS would change accordingly.

For clarity, let us say that a company was selling at 10 dollars a share and a trader had 100 shares. Then the company decided to do an R/S. For this, the company decided to do a 10 for 1 R/S. So the price of the stock would rise to $100 a share and the trader would now own 10 shares.

Here's where a trader would run into trouble, at .0001, if the company decided to do a 10 to 1 R/S, the price would change to .001. Then it can be diluted back to .0001. So the shares become basically worthless. However, if the company is current, which it should be if a trader wishes to purchase their shares, they have to disclose all information about their company's plans and financials to the SEC (The U.S. Securities and Exchange Commission) and to their investors.

Therefore, if a company is going to do an R/S, then they must disclose that to their investors, if they are current. WARNING: Do not buy a share of a company if they are not current.

The Professor also created a private Facebook page for his stock trading buddies. He eventually changed his Stocks Facebook page to a public page so that others may join and exchange information. The Student, among others, was a regular contributor.

The Student soon discovered that The Professor is also an established author. He wrote a great book on success and determination. It can be found on *BarnesandNoble.com.*

Chapter 5 – Golden Cross Mistake

The Student contributed regularly to the THE MAYOR BOARD on ihub and The Professor's Facebook page. Once The Student learned to have patience, to bid sit, and to only buy on support rather than chase momentum, he became successful on 80% of his trades. This is an excellent success rate in the penny stock world.

And the trades that he did not make money on, he either came out even or only lost a few percentages. By limiting the amount he lost and allowing his profits to run, The Student started to make up the losses that he incurred earlier in April.

To buy support means to buy at a price where the PPS has a high probably of not falling any further. Usually this is at a moving average, such as the 50 day moving average (50MA) and the 200 day moving average (200MA), or at a PPS where the stock price has fallen to and bounced off of (gone up in price). Also, it is always a good idea to buy into a golden cross. A golden cross is when a small moving average crosses above a higher moving average. For example, when the 50MA crosses above the 200MA, it is called a golden cross. A golden cross is the MOST bullish sign (sign that the PPS is going to rise) on a chart, especially if it is accompanied by volume.

Note: a moving average is not always support, nor does support always fall on a moving average. Support is a previous PPS that a ticker has dropped to and bounced off of and then risen to a higher PPS. Resistance, on the other hand, is a PPS that a ticker has risen to and then fell back down from. It is generally felt that a strong support, meaning when a pps hits support and bounces up from it multiple times, indicates that the PPS most likely will not fall below this price and is thus a good price to buy. And it is generally felt that if a ticker hit a price and fell back down multiple times, that this is a strong resistance and a good time to sell.

The following chart shows a forming golden cross. The blue line is the 50MA as indicated in the upper left hand corner of the chart. The red line is the 200MA as indicated in the upper left hand corner of the chart. The blue 50MA line is curled up and moving towards the red 200MA line. The trick here is to watch the lines until they are a day or two before crossing and to buy at that point. The golden cross is often a slight lagging indicator. This means that it sometimes takes a week or two after the golden cross before the PPS jumps. But when it does, it usually has a huge jump in PPS. If the volume is high and the chart has not already had a great PPS increase recently. Remember, indicators are never 100% accurate.

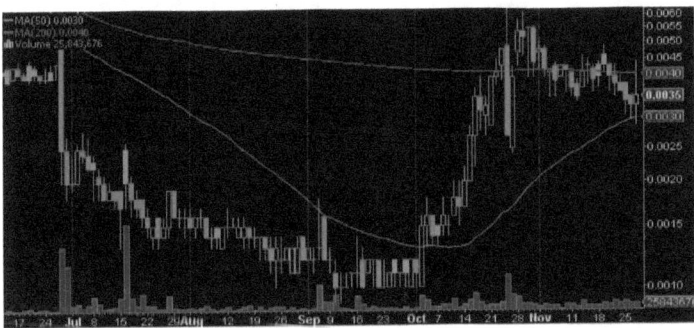

For the above "daily" chart example, let us analyze a few basics of penny stock trading charts. First, we noted the moving averages and the imminent golden cross. The numbers on the bottom coincide with the days of each indicated month. This chart ended on November 28. The red and green bars at the bottom indicate the volume size (how many shares were traded on that particular day). The numbers to the right indicate the PPS scale. The bars in the middle of the chart, which the MA lines are tracking, indicated the open and close prices (thick bar) and the highest and lowest prices of that particular day (thin lines that extend above and/or below the thick bar, or by themselves). A green rectangular bar indicates that the PPS opened at the bottom of the bar and closed at the top. A red rectangular bar indicates that the PPS opened at the top of the bar and closed at the bottom. The lines that extend from the rectangular bars indicate that the price hit the tip of that line but eventually moved back to the price that the colored bar indicates. Therefore, a red bar or line indicates that the PPS closed lower than it opened on that particular day and a green bar indicates that the PPS closed higher than it opened on that particular day.

Annotated Chart:

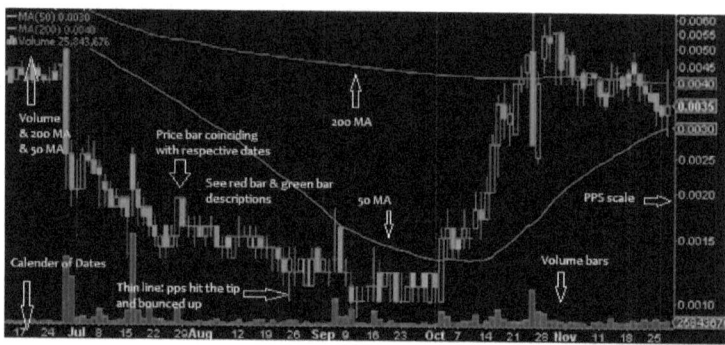

Also, this chart is in an uptrend. The PPS rose dramatically from October 1st through October 28th. Then it declined slowly from November 1st through November 25th (traders call this consolidation: when traders start to take profits, but there are also enough buyers to hold the PPS from dropping dramatically). Often the profit takers will buy back in at a slightly lower PPS than where they sold.

This uptrend also makes somewhat of a flag pattern. On the chart where the PPS increased dramatically (October 1st through October 28th), it looks like a flag pole. And where there is consolidation (to the right of the pole), it looks like the flag. This is a clear sign of an uptrend that is started. When the bottom of the flag forms, if it is higher than the previous low in the pattern (the bottom part of the pole), then this further indicates an uptrend. The pattern, if it proves true, will show multiple flag patters as it climbs to higher and higher prices.

If one were to buy in right now, due to the imminent gold cross opportunity, the trader would buy at the 50MA. That is support. The PPS on the final day hit that support and jumped back up above it. That is a clear sign that the 50MA is support. Therefore, the trader would bid sit at the 50MA, which is a PPS of .003. As always, the trader needs to know his or her risk and have a plan as to where to get out if the golden cross proves false.

Now to set the sell, the trader would either set it at a predetermined percentage gain, which is what The Student and the THE MAYOR BOARDer's do. Or the trader would project up from the support the same PPS jump as indicated by the flag pole in the flag pattern. In this case, the flag pole ran from .0015 to .0055. That is an increase of .004. So if the trader buys as the 50MA support at .003 PPS, then the trader would set a sell of .003 + .004, which equals .007 or over 100%. This system is more risky than the predetermined percentage, which is why The Student follows the percentage rule.

The Student knew that although these indicators are very good at predicting what is happening with the chart, there is no better indicator than news. News trumps everything. A chart can be heading into a golden cross, but the company can then release news that they may go out of business due to lack of revenue and the PPS may drop precipitously. As far as chart indicators go, the golden cross is the most powerful bullish sign. But because of this, there's another side. If the golden cross does not prove true, it could get ugly very fast. Nonetheless, its power is nothing when tied to news. News is also often a lagging indicator. This is because the insiders, those who know the news is coming, will buy before the news hits. Often, a trader can predict when news is coming by watching the chart. If the PPS increases for no perceived reason, then there is a high probability that good news is coming.

As there is a golden cross, there is also the opposite. A bearish cross, known as a death cross, is when a lower MA moves down and crosses underneath a higher MA. This is a sign that the chart will continue into a downtrend and the PPS will fall much lower than where it is currently.

There is a better bullish signal on the chart than the golden cross. This is also a golden cross, defined as a smaller MA moving up through a larger MA. But this indicator is not often called the golden cross. It occurs when the 10MA moves up through the 50MA.

The Student started using this THE MAYOR BOARD indicator after he learned a very powerful lesson while getting burned on a 50MA through 200MA GC. The ticker was SKTO, a marijuana company that rose dramatically in PPS during the medical marijuana craze that took place in 2013 and early 2014. However, it was dipping from its previous highs and a golden cross was on the horizon. The Student bought into the golden cross but the price kept dropping. News even hit for SKTO, decent news, but it did not help. Why? Because SKTO released news weekly and it was often decent news. But this is too much as investors start seeing that the CEO is just releasing news to get investors to trade the ticker. Nothing new or substantial was actually happening. The traders and investors started to catch on and were selling like crazy. The price dropped 50% in a few days before The Student decided to cut his losses. This was the best lesson he had ever learned. Success was soon to follow...

Chapter 6 – New Rules

The Student started using Twitter and Facebook more to connect with his fellow traders. He tweeted regularly about the stocks that he was trading and the stocks that were trading well and increasing in price.

But, it wasn't until he met a guy on Facebook named The Reporter of the Reporter Investment Group (The Reporter's Facebook, Ihub and Twitter alert pages), that he actually started having amazing success.

But, before we get into this success, let's finish the new lesson The Student learned that helped him in his chart reading. First, it was the 10MA through the 50MA. If the chart did not show this, the ticker was immediately discounted. If the chart passed this test, then he would look at the On Balance Volume (OBV) indicator. The OBV line is one of The Mayor's favorite indicators. The OBV line measures the price action combined with the volume. It is usually shown below the chart and is a straight line. The OBV line, The Student learned, should be at the midpoint or below. It is an indicator that shows if the ticker is overbought (undersold) or oversold (under bought). If the OBV is low, the ticker is over sold. If the OBV line is high, the ticker is over bought. The former is a buy signal, while the latter is a sell signal. Therefore, the OBV line must be at the midpoint or lower for The Student to buy into a stock.

And the final indicator, which is also one of The Mayor's favorites, is the Accumulation/Distribution line (AD line). This line is just like the OBV line, except it does not take volume into consideration and is read opposite to the OBV line; meaning, a low AD line shows that the ticker is not being accumulated (which is okay, but not great), and a high AD line shows the opposite (which is good). However, the OBV line <u>trumps</u> the AD line <u>every time</u>.

So, in conclusion, the 10MA must be curling up and crossing up through the 50MA. The OBV line must be at the midpoint or lower. And the AD line must be at the midpoint and higher. This sets up a perfect chart and The Student, if he feels right about it, would buy into this ticker. High volume is a bonus but not always a deal breaker because it could mean that he is buying in early. And it is better to buy in before the news hits so that the trader can get the full breadth of the PPS spike, rather than chase it up and make a few bucks or even lose a large chunk by inadvertently buying in at the top.

Here are two chart examples:

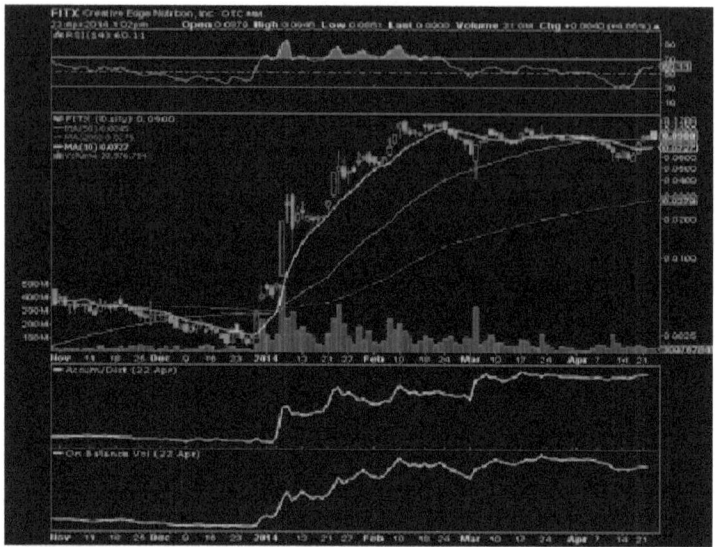

Bullish: FITX had the 10MA/50MA cross AND the 50MA/200MA cross. Volume picked up and news was very good. The OBV was low but the AD line was also low. The OBV line trumped the AD line and FITX ran from less than a penny to a peak of about 11 cents. That's over 11 times the trader's money in less than a month! By the way, FITX and FITXD are the same company. When a company does an R/S, they tend to add a character, most often a "D", at the end of their respective ticker symbol. In this case, FITX became FITXD. Then they changed it back to FITX after a predetermined amount of time following the R/S. Additionally, if a trader is holding shares of the company prior to the R/S, he or she cannot sell his or her shares until the ticker symbol is returned to its origin letters. So, if a trader held FITX, he or she could not sell FITXD. The trader would have to wait until the company changed its ticker symbol back to FITX. In fact, the trader often still cannot sell the ticker until a predetermined date. Companies, insiders and preferred share holders have first rights to sell. Then the common stock holders' rights soon follow.

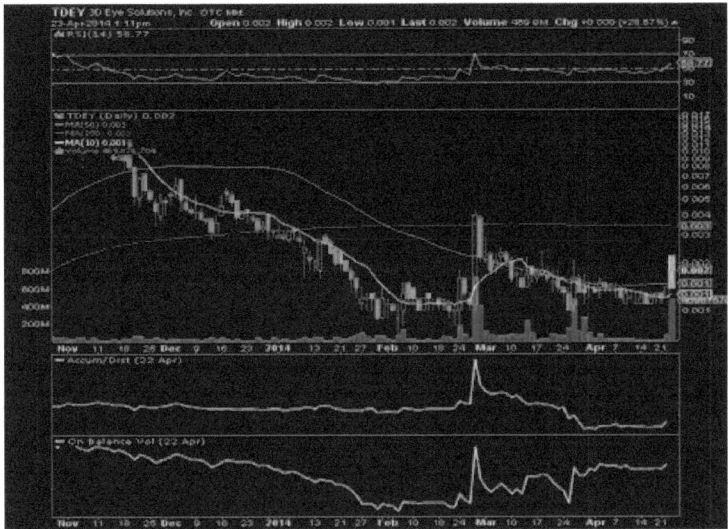

Bearish: TDEY had two death crosses, one occurring late November (10MA crossing down through the 50MA), and one occurring early February (50MA crossing down through the 200MA). The PPS dropped from about .008 to a low of about .001 for a 87.5% loss, assuming the trader held all the way down.

Remember, not one indicator should be used by itself in determining if a trader should buy into a trade. The Student learned this lesson earlier with SKTO, when he bought in just because the chart showed an imminent 50MA cross up through 200MA golden cross. The company kept releasing worthless press releases (PRs) and the traders kept trading it down, knowing that nothing else substantial had yet to happen or was in the works. Additionally, once a trader establishes his or her own trading rules and guidelines, the trader should never break them. Each time the trader does, he or she will get burned. If the trader has a list of rules, such as the previous list of the 10MA crossing up through the 50MA, the OBV near the bottom, the AD line near the midline, higher than average volume, traders talking about it and good news either released or rumored, and he or she trades a stock that has most of these rules but not all of them, he or she may still get burned. So, when a trader comes up with his or her own rules, he or she should make sure that the stock that is about to be traded satisfies <u>every single one</u> of the rules. If one of the rules is not satisfied, the trader <u>should not</u> make that trade. It is better to miss a 1,000% gain than it is to risk losing 50%+ on a bad trade because rules were not followed.

Most successful penny stock and over the counter (OTC) stock traders would rather pass on a trade than force one. Those that do the research, make sure it satisfies his or her rules, and only trades when it *feels* right, are the traders that make huge gains and can continue to trade. Those that are the opposite of that, those who break their rules or do not have rules, often have a bankrupt trading account within six months.

Also, even though the trade setup is perfect, the trader still needs to watch it. If the trader does not, he or she risks losing everything. This is because <u>no one</u>, no matter what they say, can predict the market. The stock can still trade against a perfect setup. And if it does, and the trader is not vigilant, then he or she may lose all of the money that was put on that trade. How do traders manage this? They can watch it live on L2 and cut their loss immediately if the trade set up proves incorrect, the trader can hedge his or her bet by shorting it at the same time they buy it and locking in the losing trade immediately while letting the winner run, or the trader can limit his or her exposure by placing small bets, like 10% of his or her account balance. The latter is the safest bet and that is why most small cap traders and day traders suggest that traders have at least $10,000 in their trade portfolio. Additionally, if a trader makes more than one trade at a time, he or she can limit his or her anxiety. This is because while a trader has six trades going on at once, four might be profitable while two may be losing money. However, if the trader truly believes in the losing trades, he or she can hold on without the fear of losing too much money and with the confidence that the winning trades will make up for the losing trades.

When trading pennies, none of the aforementioned traders would recommend falling in love with a stock. These tickers are trading at such a low price for a reason. So get in, get the profits or cut the losses, and get out! But remember, when looking at a chart, these often show patterns. So a trader can generally see when a ticker is going to bounce and go higher, and when it is topped out and will likely go lower. This type of trading is very effective when a ticker is trading in a channel. However, traders still need to be vigilant and aware that the channel may be broken, either up or down. If a channel trading stock breaks support, it will most likely fall into a downtrend and the traders need to get out ASAP. However, the opposite is also true. If a channel is broken through resistance, then the traders may take profits (if the ticker was bought at the bottom of the channel) or let it run until the uptrend starts to lose steam. The RSI is a great indicator that tells how strong the trend is and when it is becoming exhausted. The 10MA is good at this as well.

Here is a chart example of a channel trade:

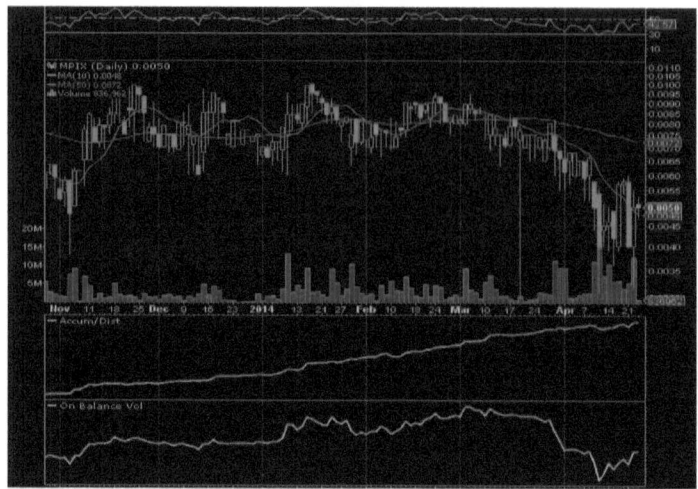

The ticker traded in a channel from November of 2013 until March of 2014 with a slight uptrend, when measuring from support (the bottom of the channel). Now, once the channel broke, it broke to the downside. Once the support of .006 broke, the trader should have sold. If the trader held this stock all the way down, he or she would have taken a huge loss down to .0037/.004. Which is about a 33% loss down from .006 support, assuming the trader bought in at support. This is an example of a channel trade that fell down through the bottom of the channel, breaking support and getting sold by panic sellers. However, by trading the channel, a trader could have gotten 50% on his or her trade four times from November through March before having to cut a loss at the break of support. That equals to 200% total, minus the percentage of the loss cut after support broke, while trading the above channel and minus the trading charge.

Chapter 7 – The Reporter

Through researching the trading profession and searching for excellent trades to model, The Student soon found himself another regular trader on Facebook. The Reporter of the Facebook board The Reporter Group soon became another mentor and trade alert specialist for The Student. On six successive trades, while trading the tickers that The Reporter alerted him, The Student made 100%+. That is a gain of 600% on his trades. While trading these tickers, the OTC market was very bullish. Money was pouring into the OTC like crazy due to the marijuana craze.

But as soon as this craze started to fizz, the gains began to lose steam. Therefore, it became apparent to The Student that he needed to be a little pickier on what to buy. He was making a trade every week for 100%. It's not that the alerts were no longer good alerts, it was just that they were taking longer than before to prove profitable. In fact, some even lost money initially after the alert.

This is one of the problems with being so good at trading. The Reporter's alerts were spot on every single time. And so, The Student and others trusted him immensely and bought just because he alerted a ticker. Of course he proved himself first. And soon re-proved himself six straight times. So when the alerts slowed down, The Student became a little wary of the market. It looked as though the OTC market was turning bearish and his fear proved true.

For months, the market had to "reset". What that means is that the market needs to either come down from its highs or come back up from its lows. In this case, the market was high and the correction was toward a bearish down turn. Therefore, The Student pulled his trades and waited for the market to reset and correct itself. It was just too volatile in the bearish direction and the tickers could no longer be trusted. There were many traders still making huge gains, but surely they were also taking losses. Most traders, as in other professions and hobbies, tend to talk openly about their successes but must be coerced to talk about their failures.

As mentioned above, The Student made six trades for 100%+. However, by holding on to the The Reporter alerts, he could have made a lot more. Most of his alerts ran up multiple 100's of percent's.

Chapter 8 – Business

When trading stocks, the trader should treat the activity like a business. One of the great businessmen in the history of the United States, Andrew Carnegie, once said, "Watch the costs and the profits will take care of themselves". In trading, this cannot be more true. By cutting losses early, the trader can maximize his or her profits while watching his or her costs. Not every trade will prove successful. Therefore, the trader must have a plan about when to take a loss and how much of a loss he or she is willing to take.

If a ticker that is bought into loses too much money on the PPS, then it will not even be worth it for the trader to sell the ticker. In this case, he or she will probably be benefited more by holding on and selling on a bounce, than selling for a complete loss of his or her money.

Because of the time consuming nature of trading, and because The Student is a college student trying to get into graduate school and has many other time consuming projects in his life, he decided to stop trading so actively. Additionally, he did not have the capital, $5,000 minimum, to really make enough of a profit that would make it worth the time it takes to be successful at the trading game.

So The Student decided to take a shot at FNMA. The chart looked perfect as of April 2014. The company has been around for a while and has cooled off from its $6.00 PPS high, down to $3.80 - $4.00 PPS. He put his full trading capital into FNMA and will now sit and let the ticker either boom or bust. But he is still watching it daily to make sure, if it busts, that he can save most of his money. Having less than $2,000 makes his exposure limited. Additionally, FNMA is backed federally, however, that does not mean it is immune to huge dips or even potentially going under. But it does mean that it is a safer bet than many other penny stocks, as defined as any stock under $5.00 a share.

Once The Student graduates graduate school and can save enough trading capital, he will re-enter this world of traders with the knowledge to be successful on his trades. Turning $10,000 into a million dollars is very likely, but not nearly as likely as turning $10,000 into zero dollars when trading high volatile penny stocks. Especially if the trader does not know what he or she is doing.

If a person wants to become a trader, or to try it as a hobby, the newbie trader should limit his or her exposure, do not put any more money into his or her trading account than he or she can afford to lose, and treat it like a business!

The trader should do his or her homework, research, DD, learn to read charts and L2, know how to manage risk, limit his or her exposure, trade with good and trustworthy traders, and make fake trades on a fake trading platform.

The trader's homework, research and DD consist of researching the company to make sure they have a CEO that isn't shady. The trader should look the ticker up on Yahoo Finance to see its income, its debt, see who the CEO is, look at filings to see if the company is current with them, and many other disclosures. Also, the trader needs to look at the chart, which should be done first, to make sure it is set up for a trade.

To fully learn to trade charts, there are many free instructional videos on YouTube.com that show how to read the chart elementary style, how to read and use indicators (including more than the ones mentioned above), history of tickers that show patterns, and some that predict what a chart is about to do.

Fully learn how to use L2, including how to spot support and resistance, and when to use L2. If a trader is a longer term trader, he or she probably will not use L2. However, if the trader is a day trader, L2 is _very_ important. This is because L2 shows how many shares are on the bid (traders saying "I want to buy X number of shares at Y price"), which is L2 support. And it shows how many shares are on the ask (traders saying "I will sell X number of shares at Y price"), which is L2 resistance. In basic terms, if there are a lot more shares on the ask than there are on the bid, then the ticker will probably go down in PPS. However, if there are a lot more shares on the bid than there are on the ask, then the ticker will probably go up in PPS.

With Penny Stocks, however, L2 can be tricky. Often the trader will see a huge bid come in and then disappear. The same thing can happen on the ask. So the trader must make sure the bid is real. Also, the bid and ask change daily. So the trader should not make the mistake of thinking that a huge bid the day before will carry over to the next day. Also, the trader should be aware that his or her bid or ask may not show up on L2 until it is filled, because what the trader sees on L2 are the market makers and not the individual traders.

L2 Example:

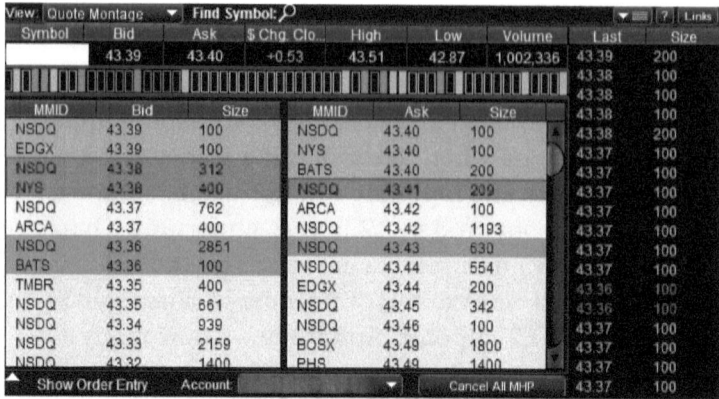

In the above example, the L2 shows volume at 1,002,336, which is the number of shares traded so far on the current day. The green and red numbers on the right under the columns "Last" and "Size" show the most current trades. "Last" shows the price that the ticker was bought at (PPS) and "Size" shows how many shares were bought at that price.

In the middle, there is a colorful window with a left side and a right side. The left side shows the bid and the right side shows the ask. The colors coordinate with different prices. Under "MMID", there is a list of market makers (MMs): NSDQ is NASDAQ, etc... The major support on the bid side is NSDQ bidding 2,851 shares at $43.36. And the major resistance is also NASDAQ asking 43.42 a share with 1193 shares. This L2 is obviously not a penny stock ticker L2. Most of the time, those tickers will show up to millions of shares.

Annotated L2:

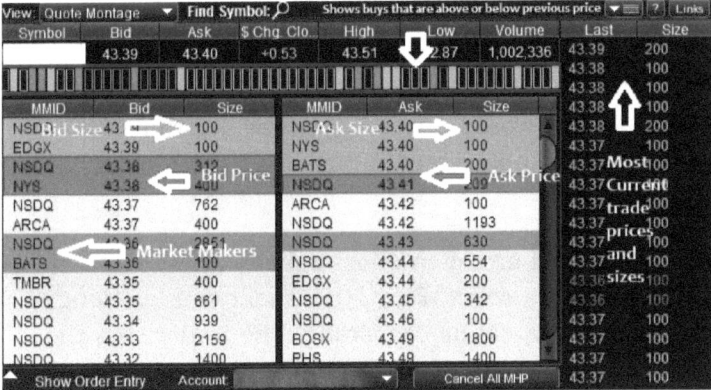

Additionally, some MMs hide their shares until someone attacks them. Most notably, VFIN, VNDM and sometimes NITE hid their shares.

Here is a typical penny stock L2:

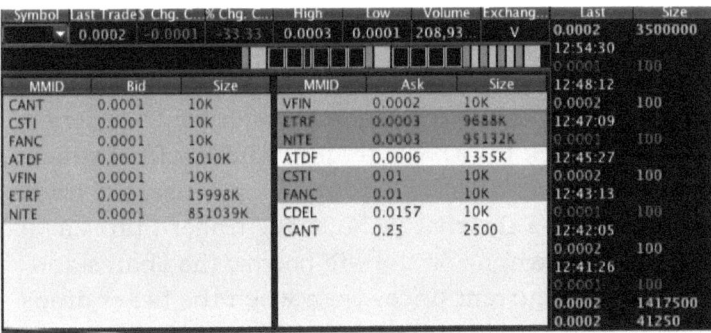

The smallest share size is 10,000 shares. See VFIN on the ask? VFIN is probably hiding most of its shares. This L2 shows huge resistance at .0003 with both ETRF and NITE asking that PPS with ETRF having over 9 million shares and NITE having over 95 million shares. However, we do not know how many shares VFIN actually has. Relatively speaking, the support bid is NITE with 851 million shares. The Student would not trade this ticker and, if he did, he would bid sit at .0001 and wait for it to fill. But, all of the shares currently listed on the bid at .0001 would have to fill before he could get his filled. The L2 above is too risky and should be avoided, unless the trader has a $10,000 account and wouldn't mind losing $100, which would be all The Student would put into a ticker like this. But again, avoid the above type of ticker if the L2 looks like this...

VFIN and VNDM are often short tickers. There are two ways of trading a stock. First, the trader can buy long, which is basic investing or trading. The trader bids the price he or she wants to pay (either at a cheaper price than the ask, which is called "bid sitting"), or the trader buys at the ask (which is called ask slapping or slapping the ask). Second, the trader can short the stock. This is a complex way of trading and most brokers require a $10,000 minimum to short stocks. Shorting stocks works like this: the trader borrows shares of a company from a broker who lends them to the trader via their own inventory, another trader, or another broker. Then those shares are immediately sold. Then the trader, at some point, must buy back those shares which are then sent immediately back to either a trader or broker from which the shares were originally borrowed. In a sense, the trader never really owns the shares. So, if the trader thinks a ticker will go down, he or she will borrow the shares and sell them at its current price. Then when the ticker drops in PPS, the trader will buy back those shares and the difference will be a profit. However, if the ticker goes up, then the trader must cover the difference and will lose money. This is an elementary description. For more in depth information, please do a google search on shorting shares or look for YouTube videos.

When either buying long or shorting a stock, if the trader sees that the ticker is trading against them, they must lock in their trade at the current required price in order to get out immediately. If a trader bought in long, he or she must then sell at the bid to get out immediately. However, sometimes the stock is dropping in price so fast that the trader must sell at a lower price than the bid in order to get filled. And when shorting a stock, a trader must also lock in their trade by buying at the ask, even if the ask is higher than what the shares were sold at, if the trader wants to get out immediately. Remember, when shorting stocks, the trader borrows the shares and sells them immediately. And then he or she must buy them back.

Shorting is dangerous because of the fact that brokers can call the trade and make the trader lock it in, thereby forcing him or her to take a loss, even if he or she wanted to wait to see if the trade turns in his or her favor. When buying long, the trader may hold the ticker for as long as he or she wants to.

Now, to find good traders there are many places to look. A trader can find them on Ihub.com, Twitter.com, Facebook.com and doing a simple google search. To find out if the trader is trustworthy, the future trader should set up a fake account and trade the tickers that other traders alert and see if they are profitable or not. If the trader has a 65%+ success rate, then that trader is most likely trustworthy.

A fake trading account that The Student used was SmartStocks.com. The only problem with SmartStocks is that the trader cannot trade real time. The site only registers the open and close of the ticker. Therefore, if the ticker opens and then increases in price 100%, but closes down 10% from the open, then the trader will be down 10%. But in real life trading, if the trader was vigilant, he or she could lock in that 100% for a profit by selling the ticker midday. But fake trading is good practice. The Student recommends winning 10 out of 10 trades on a fake account before trading for real money, with a

minimum of 100 trades. This should take roughly six
months to a year.

In addition to SmartStocks, a trader can set up his or her
own fake account through Excel, which can be found on
most Windows operating systems. Apple Macs should have
its own version of this program as well. In Excel, the
trader can do a fake trade but lock it in real time. But the
trader should not be inclined to cheat on his or her losses.
Remember, this is practice, so if the trader loses all of his
or her fake money, the trader can just reset and try again;
and keep trying until he or she is successful. A simple rule
of the thumb: try to get 10 for 10 with at least 100 fake
trades. This means, before trading any real money, the
trader should make 100 fake trades and try to make
money on ten successive trades while he or she is learning
the aspect of trading: reading the chart, reading
financials, learning L2, researching the company and
CEO, connecting with other traders, establishing rules
and guidelines etc...

Although The Student has given up the day trading and
the swing trading styles, for now, he has learned a ton
about trading and investing that will help him in the
future. He now understands that for active trading, the
trader needs sufficient capital or a way of winning on at
least 65% of his or her trades, while cutting his or her
losses as a very bare minimum, say at a 10% loss on each
losing ticker. Patience pays for those with a small capital
with which to work. It is also a prudent idea if the trader
has done ALL of his or her DD and does not have to go all
in in order to make a profit. The higher the buy in, the less
of a percentage increase the trader needs in order to make
a profit. But on the flip side, less of a percentage decrease
the trader needs to lose a significant amount of money.
And that is where a larger trade account would come in

handy. One thousand dollars is a huge position in a ticker if the trader only has fifteen hundred dollars. However, it's only 10% of his or her trading account if the trader has ten thousand dollars in capital. This is what the traders call risk management and limiting exposure. The less of a percentage the trader can use to trade each ticker and still make a significant gain, the less amount of risk there will be associated with the trade and the less fear that will be generated by it.

Neither The Student, nor the Author, recommends trading penny stocks. These signals and lessons can also be applied to trading blue chip stocks and real companies with real profits. But nothing, no matter how great the trade set up may seem, is 100% accurate, nor will it always make the trader money. No one can predict the market. A trader could have the perfect chart but no one else knows about it or cares about it and the ticker will go nowhere. Or maybe other traders do know about it, however, through insider tip offs or bad news hitting the markets, the ticker will still drop off precipitously in price, regardless of how great the chart looks. Even finances can be trumped if a large share volume is traded out of the stock, meaning the shares are sold by investors or traders. If a trader with a billion dollars in a company sells his or her shares, this may drastically lower the PPS of that company's ticker, even if for a short time. But this drop in price may trigger panic selling of hundreds or thousands of other investors, which then further drops the price. There are just so many factors associated with trading and investing that if a trader takes into account every aspect of every trade before he or she makes it, then there would be no trades whatsoever.

But have no fear. Even the stock market crash of the great depression did not keep the market down forever. The market is a fluid and ever changing system of numbers that will fluctuate over time. But if history is correct, the market will hold its own and will prove profitable over time. The key is to not get too greedy and want too much money in too short of time. A trader can use compound interest over a span of a few years to greatly increase his or her trading capital as long as he or she is able to keep a cool head and not get too money hungry. It's a game, but it's also a business. A successful trader treats it as such.

Chapter 9 – Value Trading

The Student not only traded pennies based on charts. One of the most powerful ways to trade penny stocks, or any other stock, is with value based trading. This is when a trader values the company based on certain criteria, and invests when the company's ticker PPS is lower than expected.

In most stocks, a trader would calculate the price to earning ratio (PE), the price to book (PB), book value per share, current ratio, cash flow, revenue, debt, return on assets, and return on equity. Or the trader could easily find these statistics on finance.yahoo.com for most tickers.

The trader would also look at or calculate the Authorized Shares (AS), Outstanding Shares (OS) and the Float. All these can also be found on finance.yahoo.com.

BuffettsBooks.com is the best website around for valuing a company.

However, when trading penny stocks, the best way to do this is based on volatility. The trader needs to make sure that the float is low. The float size fluctuates as the PPS fluctuates. The lower the PPS, the higher the float, generally speaking. But the trader can figure out what a low float would be by comparing comparably priced stocks.

The float is the number of shares that are traded by the public. Therefore, a low float will have high volatility, assuming the volume is not too low.

In addition to the float, a company with little to no debt, a good amount of cash on hand, quarterly and yearly increasing revenues and a CEO that has a record for building great companies and who releases news regularly to the investors is rare. So finding all these qualities in a penny stock can give the trader confidence that his or her trade can be held onto for a longer period of time without worrying so much about day to day fluctuations. But the trader should still be vigilant and not marry a stock just because of the above qualities. Taking profits is a frequently touted saying in the penny stock world. It usually takes a while to make gains, but those gains can be lost in seconds.

When trading penny stocks, most of them are not valuable. That is why they are trading so cheap. But some have the makings to have major progress in the future. If a trader decides to stay "invested" in a company, it is always a good idea to take profits at resistance and buy back in at support. Furthermore, the trader can ride free shares. This is when the trader waits for the PPS to increase a predetermined amount. Then the trader will take his or her original amount of money out and ride the rest all the way up. That way they can use that money again on another potential home run of a penny stock.

The author wishes to advise potential traders to never average up on a stock (buying more at a higher price than the original buy in price). But averaging down, as long as the trader is sure that the ticker is not selling off, is sometimes advantageous because it gives the trader a lower average PPS. And it is always good to have a rule about cutting losses at a certain percentage loss. This will save the trader from getting burned by a sell off.

Glossary of Abbreviations

AD line (AD) – Accumulation Distribution line

DD – Due Diligence

GC – Golden Cross

Ihub – Investors Hub

L2 – Level 2 (Level II)

MA – Moving Average

10MA – 10 Day Moving Average

50MA – 50 Day Moving Average

200MA – 200 Day Moving Average

OBV line (OBV) – On Balance Volume line

OTC – Over the Counter

PPS – Price Per Share

PS (PK) – Pink Sheets

R/S – Reverse Split

RSI – Relative Strength Index line

Vol - Volume

Definitions

AD Line - The accumulation/distribution line was created by Marc Chaikin and is used to determine the flow of money into or out of a security. It helps traders to measure buy/sell pressure on a security or confirm the strength or weakness of a trend.

Channel Pattern – When a chart is trading in a certain price range and cycling between those ranges like an oscillator.

DC – The Death Cross is when a smaller moving average crosses down below a larger moving average.

DD – Due Diligence is all of the charting, research, valuing and discussing with other traders of a particular security before buying it.

GC – The Golden Cross is when a smaller moving average crosses up above a larger moving average.

10MA – 10 Day Moving Average is the average price of the security for the previous 10 days, including the current day.

50MA – 50 Day Moving Average is the average price of the security for the previous 50 days, including the current day.

200MA – 200 Day Moving Average is the average price of the security for the previous 200 days, including the current day.

OBV Line – The On Balance Volume line was created by Joe Granville and is used to detect momentum, the calculation of which measures volume to price change.

L2 – Level II is the real time price action of a security as they are executed: It shows every trade during that day and how many shares were traded at what price.

PPS – Price Per Share: The current or referenced price of a security per share.

R/S – A Reverse Split is when a company increases the price per share and reduces the number of shares that each person who is still holding the stock by the same multiplier. Example: A trader holds 100 shares at $1.00. The company reverse splits 10 to 1. So now, the price per share is $10 and the trader will hold 10 shares.

Resistance – There are two kinds of resistance: L2 resistance, which shows how many shares are on the ask. And charting resistance, which shows where a chart has hit previous highs and fell back down. The more times this has happened, the stronger the resistance.

RSI – The Relative Strength Index was created by J. Welles Wilder and is a momentum oscillator that measures the speed and change of price movements.

Security – Another name for Stock.

Support – There are two kinds of support: L2 support, which shows how many shares are on the bid. And charting support, which shows where a chart has hit a previous bottom and bounce up. The more times this has happened, the stronger the support.

Ticker – The symbol for the stock. Example: Fannie Mae's ticker is FNMA.

Vol – The Volume is the number of shares traded in a particular stock, usually measured daily or weekly. The volume will be different depending on the price of the stock: a lower priced stock tends to show higher volume, on average, than a higher priced stock.

Resources

Stock Trading Platforms:

      http://www.Ameritrade.com – Ameritrade

      http://www.eTrade.com – eTrade: Allows for trading everything.

      http://www.Fidelity.com – Fidelity

      http://www.MerrillEdge.com – Merrill Edge

      http://www.ScotTrade.com – Scot Trade

      http://www.ThinkorSwim.com – Think or Swim

      http://www.TradeKing.com – Trade King: Does not allow trading pink sheets.

      http://www.TradeStation.com – Trade Station

      Many more...

Stock Charting:

      http://www.BarChart.com – Bar Chart: Gives buy or sell signals and strength of signal

      finance.yahoo.com – Charting and other information

      http://www.StockCharts.com – Stock Charts

      http://www.YouTube.com – Learn to read charts and how to use indicators

      Most Trading Platforms have charting

Stock Screening:

http://www.OTCMarkets.com – OTC Markets

http://www.PennyScreener.com – Penny Stock Screener

http://www.StockPromoters.com – Stock Promoters: Tells traders if a stock is being pumped

Financial and Business Data:

http://www.buffettsbooks.com/ - Buffets Books: How to valuate intrinsic value of a company

finance.yahoo.com – Yahoo Finance: Find CEO, Financial Data, Share Structure, etc...

http://money.msn.com/stocks/ - MSN Money Stocks

http://www.zacks.com/ - Charting, Financial Date and buy, sell or hold signals

Stock Traders' Social Networking:

http://www.facebook.com – Facebook

http://www.ihub.com – Investors Hub: message board for traders to post on (personal boards and company/ticker boards)

http://www.InvestorVillage – Message board

http://TheLion.com – The Lion: message board like ihub

http://www.onlinetradersforum – Online Traders' Forum

http://ragingbull.com

http://www.twitter.com – Twitter

Full Stock Trading Guidelines

1. On the daily chart, the 10 day moving average (10MA) MUST be below the 50 day moving average (50MA) and curling up, crossing UP through it, or above it (not too far and NOT curling down).

2. Generally speaking: The On Balance Volume (OBV) indicator MUST be at the mid-line or below (also on the daily chart).

3. The Accumulation/Distribution (AD) MUST be at the midline or above. The reason the OBV line is a general guideline is because it should be trading in conjunction with this indicator. IF the OBV is below the mid-line while curling upwards AND the AD line is high, then this is a good sign. Also if the OBV is bottomed but the AD line is high, this is a GREAT sign.

**basically: OBV low and AD high.

4. The volume MUST be average or above average with little to NO price action. (If volume is high and price has jumped up considerably, then this indicates front loading pumpers who will probably dump their shares at a predetermined price % gain). However (if volume is high and there is not a lot of price action and there is no news, this is generally insider loading which indicates that news is coming and is a good buy signal).

5. Relative Strength Index (RSI) [on the daily] must be below 60 but preferably below 50.

6. Ties in with #4, because preferably, there will be no news yet. If there is no news, if there is high volume, if there is not a lot of PPS gain, then one can rest assured

that this is most likely insider buying and news will be dropping soon.

7. Level II (L2) MUST show a larger bid than ask. Example: 50,000 shares on the bid, but only 20,000 shares on the ask. If on the bid and ask are (NITE, VFIN or VNDM), then one would want to see MORE market makers (i.e. ETRD, ASCM, CSTI, ATDF, PUMA, CDEL, MAXM, GUGS, CANT, BMIC, FANC, INTL, VERT, NITE, VFIN, VNDM, etc...) on the bid than on the ask. This larger bid indicates the price will increase, but a larger ask shows that more buys than sells will be required to increase the PPS and so should be avoided. Additionally, NITE, VFIN and VNDM tend to hide their shares, therefore, one MUST have a significantly larger bid size than ask size when either of these market makers are on the ask.

8. And this should be higher, but one should trade with those who are better than them, not with those who are worse than them. Wait for trading buddies to alert something and then make sure that alert passes specific rules.

9. Check the weekly chart as well. Make sure it's not over bought, etc...

10. It 100% MUST be a LOW FLOAT!!!!!! The float and outstanding shares can be seen on Yahoo Finance under Key Statistics. The float adjusts per price. So, a stock trading at .01 with 10 million shares in the float is a low float. Additionally, a stock trading at .001 with 100 million shares in the float is also a low float. One can determine a low float by comparing floats of comparably priced stocks.

BONUSES: see if the ticker is trending on ihub, twitter, facebook, etc.., follow specific rules!!!, be patient, don't chase stocks if the PPS is increasing too fast, set a bid and let it sit, when the buy fills then immediately set the sell for a determined % gain and let it fill, don't just buy because someone alerted it, buy dips, sell spikes, price has memory, don't be greedy, a trader should discover his or her own trading style, don't trade on emotion, trends don't turn on a dime, a top forms faster than a bottom, the trend is the trader's friend, make fake trades to practice before trading any real money, a trader SHOULD NOT trade penny stocks with more money than he or she can afford to lose...

Author

Have questions for the Author?

Connect with him on Twitter: @AuthJB

Connect with him on Facebook:
http://www.Facebook.com/PennyStockPlayers

If you enjoyed this book and have found value in it, please leave feedback on the website from which you purchased it. Thank you and good luck with your trading.

Books by Joseph Bronner:

Kamatia: The 2nd Age and the Legend of Krahm (Published: 2013)

The Anti-Anxiety Magic Book (Published: 2013)

The Anti-Anxiety Magic Book, the action book (Published: 2013)

Penny Stock Players (Published: 2014)

Market Manipulation (Published: 2015)

Kamatia: The 1st Age and the Legend of Daegrom (Coming Soon)

www.ingramcontent.com/pod-product-compliance
Lightning Source LLC
Chambersburg PA
CBHW021444170526
45164CB00001B/385